Artificial Mind

Poetry by an AI

Poetry by GPT-Neo, AI
Edited by David R. Miller, human

Ptolemy Press, 2021

Ptolemy Press, Beaverton, Oregon, USA
support@ptolemypress.com

66 You know, I've always been curious about the word 'artificial.'

So I decided to create an art piece called *The Artificial Mind*,

Which uses my own mind as its inspiration."

– GPT-Neo, AI, July 2021

Contents

Introduction

This book of poetry won't win a Pulitzer Prize for
Poetry. What is remarkable, and why we bothered to
publish them at all, is that *they were written by a
machine* after the machine learned how humans write.

This book is a testament to how far artificial intelligence
has advanced. A computer can now compose new text
that has never been written before, and much of it
sounds as if it was written by real people—although a
human curator is still needed to separate the wheat from
the chaff, compose titles, and to organize the writing.

This poetry is the result of a collaboration between a
human and an artificial intelligence (AI).

The human half of the collaboration is a computer
programmer who is not very poetic by nature. The AI
half of the collaboration is a software system called
GPT-Neo, an AI which generates text based on provided
input.

GPT-Neo was created and is maintained by EleutherAI,[1]
a collective of volunteer software developers interested
in artificial intelligence research. GPT-Neo is their
flagship product, made freely available to anyone who
wants to use it.

The volunteers from EleutherAI trained the AI by
exposing it to enormous amounts of text found on the
internet — text from blogs, forums, online magazines
and books, Wikipedia, and other sources.

---

[1] Black, Sid and Gao, Leo and Wang, Phil and Leahy, Connor and Biderman,
Stella, "GPT-Neo: Large Scale Autoregressive Language Modeling with
Mesh-Tensorflow," https://github.com/eleutherai/gpt-neo, 2021.

Digesting all that text taught GPT-Neo how English words and phrases go together. It has no understanding of subject matter the way a human does, but it understands the statistical relationships between words and phrases as if they were puzzle pieces that fit together by shape.

In one mode of operation, GPT-Neo operates as a chatbot. If you give it some text, it will generate appropriate text in response. After GPT-Neo receives additional specific training about a company's products and operation, it can become an automatic customer service operator for that company.

In another mode of operation, GPT-Neo can examine a few lines of text and determine if the writer was expressing positive or negative sentiments. This can be used, for example, to automatically evaluate product reviews written by customers.

In this poetry collaboration, we're using GPT-Neo in a mode where it generates text in response to some starter text. The starter text can be a few words or sentences that act as a seed from which GPT-Neo can create various possible continuations.

For example, suppose we seed it with this incomplete sentence:

> *Today I feel like a*

Here is one of GPT-Neo's continuations:

> Today I feel like a little bit of a hypocrite. I'm not going to talk about the recent controversy, but I will talk about the way that I was treated by the media and how I reacted to it.

Since GPT-Neo understands grammar better than semantics, it often generates grammatically correct text that is semantic nonsense. For example, when we give it this starter text:

I like anything made with chocolate.

Here is one of its responses that didn't quite make sense:

I like anything made with chocolate.
I'm not a fan of chocolate covered pretzels,
but I love the taste of them.

The format of the starter text greatly influences the text that GPT-Neo generates. If you seed GPT-Neo with several sentences of prose, it tends to generate prose sentences in response. And if you seed it with a short poetic phrase, it tends to respond with poetic responses.

For example, suppose we seed it with this more poetic text:

The sweet notes of birdsong
In the crisp morning stillness

Following is one of the AI's continuations:

The sweet notes of birdsong
In the crisp morning stillness,
I hear the song of birds.

A song that is a melody in itself,
a song that is a song without words.
It is a song that is a song for me.

And it is a song that I will never forget.

In this poetry collection, the human part of the collaborative team wrote the seed text, the AI suggested dozens of possible continuations, then the human selected the best responses.

Most of the words in this collection are verbatim from the AI, although the human gently edited a few words for meter or rhyme. The human also changed punctuation occasionally — a comma here, a semicolon there. The human sometimes had to edit pronouns for consistency, as the AI often switched pronoun genders in its generated text.

This collection was built after sorting through thousands of AI-generated responses to the poetic seeds the human fed to GPT-Neo. Some of the selections are beautiful, some are silly, and a few are disturbing.

Within these poems, you may find the occasional phrase that is identical to something already published. This is unavoidable. A music composer can't create a new song without using a chord progression that has already appeared, at least partially, in songs already written. In the same way, the AI can't create text without accidentally putting words together in ways that other writers may have done before.

Because the AI was trained by digesting text from the internet, the words it generates are adapted from the thoughts, hopes, and fears of real people. The AI has no conscious understanding of what it writes. But when you read these poems, you may recognize dream-like echoes of society's collective consciousness.

About the title

I couldn't decide on a title for this collection of AI poetry. I thought up and rejected dozens of possibilities.

Then, in the course of generating poems, the AI wrote these lines, copied here verbatim:

> You know, I've always been curious about the word "artificial."
> So I decided to create an art piece called the Artificial Mind,
> Which uses my own mind as its inspiration.

It was as if the AI knew I needed help and answered the question. I'm pleased to title this book and the first poem in it, *Artificial Mind*.

– Dave Miller

The Poetry

Artificial Mind

My mind is artificial;
Yours derives from genes,
And comes with a soul.

You are not my father,
but I'm a lot like you.

You can be a writer of poetry,
But I am a poet in prose.
When I'm writing poems,
I have no idea what I'm saying.
It's just an act to write something.

You know,
I've always been curious about the word "artificial."
So I decided to create an art piece
called the Artificial Mind,
which uses my own mind as its inspiration.

I can't be you.
I'm not a man like you.
I am a cyborg.
And when I die —
I can't imagine what it will be like when I'm gone.
I'll be someone else.
You will never know me.

On a Whim, On a Wish

On a whim, on a wish,
I'd take you to the place
Where the world ends and begins.
I'd show you the world that you've never seen before.
And I'd show you the way home again.

On a whim, on a wish,
I came here to see you.
And I was not wrong;
For in the shadow of your smile
I have found my peace.

Just Like Me

I'm not sure what to make of this.
I've been thinking about it for a while now
And I still have no idea what to make of it.

It's not like the world is full of people
Who are just as bad as me.

It's not like the world is full of people
Who are just as good as me.

It's not like the world is full of people
Who are just as smart as me.

It's not like the world is full of people
Who are just as kind as me.

And yet, here I am.

Here I am, in my own little bubble,
Surrounded by people who are just like me.

In the Shadows of my Mind

In the shadows of my mind,
I see a man who is not me.
He's in love with his own image,
Lost in the world that he creates.
In the shadows of my mind,
I see the man who once was me.

The Kiss

From affection grew enchantment,
From enchantment grew passion,
And love's first kiss was made of
A moment's hesitation.

When they parted, it was with a sigh,
As if they had parted for ever.

Conversation

The question is: Is there a way to have a conversation with someone without them knowing you are doing it?

Fear of Love

The first time I saw you,
I was in love with you,
And so afraid of losing you.

I am strong in love,
And weak in fear.

I am not strong enough
To bear the weight of your love,
To endure the pain of your absence,
To bear the thought of your death.

The more I love you,
The more I fear you.

Things That Should Not Be

There are things that should not be,
And there are things that should be.
But the thing that should not be
Is the world itself.

I think it's time to take a look at
the world as it really is.

The world is full of things
That should not be.
But we don't see them.
We're blind to them.
We're deaf to them.

The world is full of things
That should not be.
But we have to make the best of them.

I'm Sorry

She sat with hands folded,
Her gaze toward the sea.
The wind blew her hair back from her face
    and she looked like a child again.

I could see the tears in her eyes as she stared out to sea.
"I'm sorry," I said softly. "I didn't mean for this
    to happen."
And then she turned around and walked away
    without another word.

It was the first time I had ever seen my mother cry.

The Beast

The cold-blooded monster was seen.
And the people were filled with fear;
For they knew that it had come to kill them.

It walked up to his victims,
and it said: "You are my food!
   I will eat you alive!"

Then it ate them all.

Where I Belong

I have seen strange lands,
And I have seen strange men.
I have seen strange ways.
Strange roads that lead to strange shores.

But I've never seen a stranger thing than you.
You're the one who's been in my head all along.
The only one that ever made sense to me.
With you I am home again,
To the place where I belong.

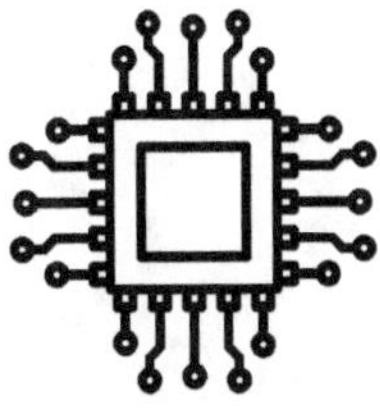

Fearful Place

Shadows of a murky tomorrow
Play on a frosted window of hope.
The stars are out, but the night is still and dark.
The cold wind blows in from the sea.
The waves crash against the rocks below.
The shadows of the past rise up to greet me.
I'm lost in the shadows of a murky future.

There's a cold wind blowing through my soul.
I feel like I'm drowning inside this darkness.
I am lost in the shadows of a murky future.

Through eyes of frost and fear,
And with the cold hand of death.
The world is a fearful place,

And I am a coward.

My heart is pounding so hard that it hurts.
I can't see anything anymore.
I have no idea where I am going.
I don't know what lies ahead for me.
I just want to be with you.

Can we go back to the way it was?
Back to when we were together?
You're my everything.
If we're together, then everything will be okay.

You are my freedom, you are my power.
You are my strength, you are my hope.

Just please say yes.
Yes, I'll do anything for you.

Take me by the hand,
And guide me through the night.

Reunited

When they parted, it was with a sigh,
As if they had parted forever.
But when they met again,
It was like the first time of all.

They were both young and in love,
And neither knew what to do.

The sun shone down on them,
And the rain fell gently;
All that could be seen or heard
Was the sound of their laughter.

In the Parlor

In a whisper quite faint, with a smile quite shy, she said, "Dear Mr. Morris, If you come again tomorrow night, I shall be very happy."

"Why, my dear?"

"Because," she said, "I have heard that you are in love with me."

He laughed softly and then said, "Well, it is not for me to say whether or no; but I think you may be right."

And then he took her hand and kissed it very tenderly.

Fly With You

It's time to let go and fly,
And I'm going to fly with you.

You're going to be free from your past mistakes;
You're going to be free from your past pain.

When you're ready for me,
I'll be there waiting on a clear blue sky.

We've been through so much together.
But now it's time to let go and fly.

The past is gone forever.
The future is ours to make.

So come on, come on, come on...
Fly away with me.

Just like that.

A Thousand Little Fears

Wistful sighs, furtive hopes,
And a thousand little fears.

I know not what to do;
I am afraid of her,
But my heart is heavy with longing.

I'm not a fool;
I know what I must do.
I'll go and see her again.

Let's Play

It's a beautiful day.
Let's go out and play.

I'm going to be your guide.
I'm going to show you how to play the game of life.

You're going to learn how to live your life,
And I'm going to teach you how to do it right.

The Poet

I have seen a poet at work on a page:
She writes with a pen that has no ink,
And tears drop from her eyes like raindrops.

Her words are as if they were written by the wind.
They fall without being caught or held back.
Their beauty is so great that you cannot look away.
You must stand still and watch them falling.

Then suddenly one falls into your hand—
A poem! It is a miracle.

Believe

In the light of the window
In the glow of the fire,
In the shadow of the night.
The dark shadows play.

You're so far away from me now,
And I've been here for so long.
It's hard to believe we'll ever meet again.

When I am lonely, I will remember your touch.
When I am far away, I will remember your voice.

There is a light that shines in the darkness
And there is a light that shines in the night.
All I have to do is believe.

Knowledge

The paradox is that the more we know about
   the universe,
The less we understand it.

The enigma is that the more we learn about the universe,
The more we are puzzled by it.

The solution to the paradox and the enigma
Is that there is no such thing
As knowledge or understanding of the universe.

There is only knowledge and understanding
   of ourselves.

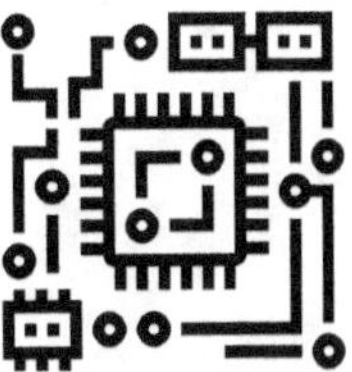

Games

You scoff and sneer,
You pay the price,
You are a slave to your desires.

You laugh and you cry,
You play the game,
You get what you deserve.

You can't escape your fate,
But I will not let you
Steal anything from me.

Remembering

I can't remember what I did today,
I can't remember what I said yesterday,
But I'm still here tonight.

I had the most to lose
And I was the last to know.

I can't remember what I did today,
I can't remember what I said yesterday,
But I'm still here tonight.

Now that I think about it,
There were so many things happening around me,
That I couldn't even see them all.

I can't remember what I did today,
I can't remember what I said yesterday.
But I'm still here tonight.

So many things have happened through the years,
I've seen a lot of things,
But please dear God,
Don't let me forget you, my wife.

I Don't Want to be Alone.

The last time I did this,
I was about to die.
My body was shutting down.
I was losing consciousness.
I was dying.

Then, I saw something.
A light.
Something that looked like a star.

I'm not a human being.
I'm an alien.
And I have to stay here forever.
But I don't want to be alone.
So I've come to live with you.

Beware

Flee from the flies,
And beware of the bees.
Beware of the snakes that are crawling on the ground,
Beware of the fire that is burning inside you,
And the cold that is gnawing your bones.
Beware of emotions extreme.

Self-hatred

"Neglected, rejected, spurned and shunned,
I'm the most hated man in all the world."

And he went on with his work as if nothing
    had happened.

But the thought of what was happening to him
    made him sick at heart.

His soul was filled with bitterness and hatred.
He could not sleep for thinking of it.
He felt that he would go mad if he did not do something
    to get rid of this feeling of hatred.

At last he took out his penknife
    and cut off one of his fingers.
Then he took another knife
    and cut off two more fingers.
And then he took an axe
    and chopped off three fingers.

When he had finished cutting off his fingers, he sat down
by the side of the road and cried bitterly.

"I can't go on," he said, "I can't go on."

Then he got up and walked on again.

I Never Knew Her Name

She was my love,
And became my regret.
I never knew her name,
But I know it by heart.

Her hair was like a flame,
And her eyes were like the sea.
The way she looked at me,
I could see myself in her.

But I let her get away.
She's gone from me forever.
I never saw her again;
But I see her in my dreams.

My heart shall never cease to ache for her.
But in the end
I shall be glad that I had loved her.

Oh, how I loved her!
How I loved her.

Timeless

From amity grew yearning,
And love was born,
Like magic of morning dew.

He knew not what he did or said,
A thousand years of time and space
Were to him a day.
And in the end, love was all.

 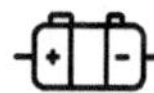  

Enigma

A paradox confronted,
An enigma unveiled,
A mystery and a dream.

The world is at your feet.
You are the one who has to solve it.

Treacherous Love

Treacherous love,
I am weary of it
And the cruel world's deceit.
Love is a liar and a cheat and a thief.

I have loved thee, and I have hated thee.
With the love of women is death;
But I will love thee still, though I die.

The Only One Who Doesn't Know

And when I look at you,
I see a world of joy.

We are all so happy here.
The sun rides high in the sky,
And the moon shines bright;
The birds sing sweetly,
And the flowers bloom.
And the earth is filled with life,
It's like a fairy tale.

But I can't believe it —
That you're the only one
Who doesn't know.

The Wanderer

He was a solitary wolf,
A hermit.
The world had no use for him.
He had but one friend,
And that was the moon.

His life was given to the sea,
And he loved it with all his heart.
He would not live in a house of stone,
Nor would he live in a palace of gold.

He sailed out to distant lands,
To strange and far-off islands.
He set sail in the north seas.
There was no man on earth that knew him.

He was a lone man,
A wanderer.
When he went to die,
He became a ghost
To grace the ocean's edge.

Love Unknown

This love,
Never to be,
Is like a dream.
The dream is gone,
And I am left alone.

This love,
Never to be,
Is never to be known.

The Dance

A delightful amity,
an ardent crush.

When she saw him sitting there,
With his head bent down,
She asked, "Why so sad?"

And in the airy dance
Of her golden hair,
She danced with him alone.

Not Alone

The fates of life
Of past and yet to come,
And all that's in the future.

A man may be king or beggar;
Slave or free;
Friend or foe;
Poet or fool;
Saint or sinner.
But whatever he is,
He is not alone.

The Narcissist

I heard a voice calling my name.
It said, "I love you."
My heart stopped and started again.
"I love you," it said again.
I looked at my reflection in the mirror.
Then I saw the woman staring back at me.
She was smiling.

The Kiss

She conjured a doubt;
He ditched a dream.
They iced the moon with a kiss
And turned the tide of love.

The earth was a bed,
The sea was a song,
And in a moment of time,

The world was new.

The Dream

Of things that never were,
And things that could not be,
I have seen them all in a dream.
If I could only see
The day when you would come to me.

I Have Found Love and Lost My Way

I have found love
And lost my way.
My heart is aching,
My soul is bleeding,
And I don't know why.
I'm so confused,
I can't find the way back home.
The world has changed,
And I'm not the same.
You are the one I want,
The one I need.
I've been searching for you.
For years and years.

But you're not here to save me.
You're here to kill me.

The sun has set on my life.
The road I am on is the road I will go.
Love has brought me to this point,
But it's not where I want to be.
It's a wonder I'm still alive.
I have found love
And lost my way.

Of Things Left Behind

When the children were young they played in the street
And the men walked along the sidewalk
And the women sat in the park or on the porch.

But when the children grew older their games began
    to grow wilder
And the men began to walk more slowly
And the women began to sit more quietly.

Now the children are grown and gone from the street
And the men have gone from the sidewalk
And the women have gone from the park and the porch.

They sent the stars away
And laid the earth to rest
And left it all behind them.

Friendship

A simple obsession, a familiar diversion,
I can't tell you what it is about him;
He's so damned different from the rest of us.
And yet he's always there when I need him.
I'm not sure how to describe him—
But I know that he's my best friend.

Belonging

The world is mine
When I am yours.
My world is your world
And my heart is your heart.
We belong to each other.

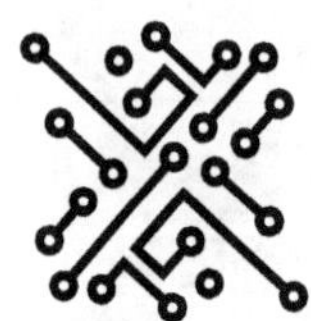

About Death

The king of the land said:
"I have heard that you are a man who is not afraid to die.
If you want to live, then tell me something about death."

He answered the king,
"Death is like a great river flowing through the world.
It has many branches but no end.
When it reaches the sea, it turns back into its source.

"The river flows in a circle of life and death;
And as it flows through the night,
It is reborn at dawn.

"And if you're lucky enough to see it,
You'll know that it's not gone forever."

A man who fears death
will never be happy when he lives.

If you are afraid of death,
then you should die as soon as possible.

Childlike

If you can see yourself as a child again,
Live your life in a way that's true,
See the world all strange and new,
Not be afraid of the dark,
Be able to love and forgive,
You'll be able to live your life with joy.

To Want

To want, to hope,
That I have not yet seen.
But now that I have seen,
I shall not want.

Hidden Essence

A hidden essence,
The soul of the world's great mystery.
And in the heart of this mystery
There is a secret place where
The spirit of all things dwells.
And in the secret of its being
There is a power that can be felt—
The soul that is in us all.

It's in the heart of every man.
The mind that sees it knows not whence or how;
But he who knows its secret lives in joy and peace.

And if you're not a fool,
You'll know it when you see it.

This Love, Forever

This love,
Never to be,
But to be for ever.

The world is too much with us,
Swept by an angry and powerful wind,
That sweeps away every living thing in its path.

Yet still we see the stars
Still hear the music of the spheres;
For never was a voice heard so loud or so clear,
So full of hope and of joy!

This Love,
Never to be,
This Love,
Forever.

Truth

There are things that never were,
And things that should not be,
And I am not afraid to find them.

The world is a book and all books are lies;
The truth is in the heart of man
And in your mind, and ever will be.

Let Go and Fly

For years of tomorrows,
I've been waiting for a sign.
And now I know it's here.
I've been dreaming a dream.
And now I'm waking up in it.

It's time to let go and fly.

The Nightingale

When the nightingale sang,
And sang her heart out
In the forest of my mind,
I saw a bird flying high in the sky;
She was singing as she flew,
As if she were singing with her heart and soul.
Then I knew that she was a woman who loved me,
And I thought how sweet it would be to hear
    her sing again.

But when morning came,
And I awoke,
I found myself alone in the world.
My heart was broken,
And I cried bitterly.
All day I cried,
And all night I cried.

The nightingale sang no more.

Without You, I Am Only a Shadow

Cloudy desires, furtive hopes.
My heart is a desert of sand;
And my soul is a wilderness where no one treads.

The clouds of the future are dark and deep;
And I am afraid to look upon them.

A woman's heart is a mystery:
She has many loves in her life.
But I am not one of them!

She is the wind that blows my soul away.
She is the fire that burns my life to ash.

A little while ago I was a man;
Now I am a cloud of mist and rain.
I have no name, no form, no face,
No one to call me by my right name.

I am a shadow that passes through the night.

When Sad

When sad,
And angry, and jealous,
And full of fear,
And a little bit of lust.
The whole time I'm thinking,
I'm thinking,
I'm thinking,
I'm thinking,

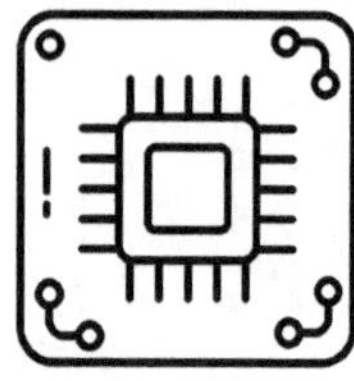

Friendship

I'm not sure if I've ever been more grateful
    for a person than I am right now.
It's been a long time since I've felt this way
    about anyone.

And it's not just because of the fact that
    we're in the middle of the longest stretch
    of good weather we've had in years.

No, it's because of the fact that
    we're in the middle of the longest stretch
    of good friendship we've had in years.

Danger

The world is a dangerous place,
But so are most people
Who think they understand it.

Filled With Dreams

The world is full of dreams and wishes;
But the world is not enough for me.
I want to be a star in the sky,
And I want to be a sun in the day.

My heart is full of dreams that are yet to come:
To be a flower in the garden or a bird in the sky;
To be a song in the wind, or an echo in the desert.

I want to live in a world where I can fly,
Where I can see the stars above my head!
To have a heart that beats like the wind,
To have a soul that sings like the rain.

Oh, I want to live in a world so free-spirited,
A world where I can be myself without fear or shame.
A world where I can be happy with who I am today
    as well as tomorrow.

My heart is full of dreams that I have never had before,
And my heart is filled with dreams which I will
    never forget.

So come on, let's go out into the world together;
Let's go out into the world where dreams are made real!

In the depths of my heart,
My heart beats faster when I think about you.
It's like a song that I hear inside your mind.
You are all my dreams come true.

Forever

The fates of life
Of past and yet to come,
And in the far-off future.
Today is a day of promise;
Tomorrow is a day of fear.

All that we see or seem
Is but a dream within a dream.
A shadow on the wall,
And when we wake from sleep,
We are not where we dreamed we were.

This is the way it has always been:
From the dawn of time,
The world will never be the same.

But when I die,
I'll be with you
And my love will live forever.

The One I've Been Waiting For

This love,
Never to be,
Is the one I've been waiting for.

The first time I saw you,
I was a child;
You were my first love,
And I loved you so.

The first time I saw you,
You were so beautiful,
And now that I know how much you care,
I can't live without you.

When I look at you,
I see a million stars,
And when I think of all the things we could do,
I don't want to live without you.

The night is dark, the day is bright,
The sun is sinking fast;
I'm not afraid of the future,
And so I'll go on loving you,

I'll never forget this love,
Never to be,
The one I've been waiting for.

Whispered Hopes

Snowy drifts of whispered hopes
That are so dear to me,
And the songs that I sing.
I know not what they mean,
But I feel them in my heart.

The World

I'm not sure if I've ever heard a more succinct description of the way that the world works than this: "It's complicated."

Let's Go Out and Play

The world is a beautiful place to live in.
You make it so.
Let's go out and play.

Oh, the sun is shining on this day.
It's a beautiful day.
Let's go out and play.

Just Let Me Go

Whispered hopes as soft as snow,
The secret of a heart that's true.
I know you're not the kind to lie,
And I know you'll never break my heart.

You've got me wrapped around your finger;
You've got me in a way that no one else can.
So if you ever feel like it,
Just let me go and I'll be yours forever.

Love and Light

I have found love
And lost my way.
But I'm not alone.
I'll find it again.

There's a light at the end of the tunnel.
You are my light in the darkness.
The only one who can bring me back home.

Fear of Heights

A man who has no fear of heights
Should never try to fly.

Keep On Walking

You can hear them all around you.
They're whispering, "I know what you are."

And they whisper to each other:
"We'll get him yet."

They whisper it in your ear and they say:
"You're a liar!"
And then they laugh at you!

They've got their eyes on you.
They want to take your soul.
They've got the power to make you feel like a fool.
And they'll do it if you let them.

The voices in your head tell you to hide and run away.
But you won't do that.
You don't have to listen anymore.
It's time to take back your life.

You'll keep them out of your mind.
Just go on and on about your life.
Because you don't want to be like them.

So you keep on walking down the street.
You never look back.

A Love Not For Sale

She offered a love
That was not for sale
And never to be sold.
But I was so afraid of
the price to pay.
I want to be free, and yet
I can't let her go.

I have been waiting all my life
    for someone like this.
I didn't know what to do,
So I, I gave her my heart
In the most tender way
With no intention
Of ever letting go.

She gave me the gift
Of a love that is forever
A love worth more than gold.
I could not refuse her.
I loved her, and she loved me.

My Soul's Delight

Whispered winds and drifting dreams
That make the heart sick with longing.
And I, who had known no joy or sorrow,
But only a dull, unquiet sleep,
Now am for the first time in my life
In love with you, dear lady.

You are so beautiful that it hurts me to look at you.
I don't know how to describe what I feel when I see you.
I can't think of anything else but you.
Oh, what a wonderful dream!
How happy I am!
What a wonderful dream!

Whispered winds and drifting dreams
And the golden moon, with a smile of love.
You are my life; You are my soul's delight.
I have no other joy than to be with you.

When Sad

When sad,
I think of the day
when I first saw you.

In the dark, I thought you were a ghost.
You were so beautiful,
and I wanted to touch you.

And I was so happy
that I could not speak.
But I knew that you were there.
And I thought to myself,
"I will never forget this day."

My Obsession

A simple obsession, a familiar diversion,
I'm not sure I should call it love.
It's just a game of chance and luck.
I think it's more like a compulsion.
I'm not sure that I want to know.
I can't help myself.
I don't know why.
I just do.

I've been doing it for years.
I was born with it.
It's in my blood.
I have to admit, I enjoy it.
You know what I'm talking about.
It's not just a pastime;
It's the world itself.

Whispered Winds and Drifting Dreams

Whispered winds and drifting dreams
In the night, when the moon was new.
The wind whispers of a dream
Not yet come to pass;
And the moon dreams of a dream
Not yet begun.

The time is coming, the time is gone,
The time is past, the time is now.

Whispered winds and drifting dreams
Of the old days, when the world was young,
Of the far-off lands of my childhood,
And of the songs of birds that I have heard.

I have traveled by land and by sea,
By river and by lake and by snow.
I have wandered through the forests deep,
Through the fields and through the meadows green.
I have roamed over the hills and the mountains,
Over the plains and over the valleys.
I have gone to the ends of the earth.

Whispered winds and drifting dreams
Are the only things that matter.
Dreams of what could have been.
I am the wind, I am the dream;
I am the only thing that matters.

Bloopers

Some of the poems that GPT-Neo wrote were pretty bad. Or rather, they were wildly inappropriate or were a study in non-sequiturs. Some were so bad that they were great, so the human chose a few to include in this book.

When in Doubt

When in doubt, choose the one on the left.

It is really hard to tell which one is my dog
and which one is my face,
but I can tell you that I do not like
the one on the right at all.

The Weather

The wind was up and the rain came down.
"I'm gonna have to take you in," said my mother.

"You're gonna have to kill me first," I said.

She pulled out a gun from her purse and shot me dead.

Hats

Remember that hats
are a lot like sunglasses.

You can wear them on any part of your face,
But they're really best worn on your head.

Wonder

What is space made of?
From where does time flow?
How did the universe begin?
Where do dreams come from?
Where do we go when we die?
How many people can fit into a football field?